"Think of Joan Jett crashing the Miss America pageant and reading her poems for the talent competition! And winning! It's deus ex machina on adrenalin. How refreshing to read a book that fills the modern world with mystery once again. Erin Keane's first book helps us 'find the coiled infinite inside' so that we end up fluent in the pure language of awe."

—RANE ARROYO, author of *The Portable Famine* and winner of the John Ciardi Poetry Prize

"With a confident and alert use of language, this poet sets out to discover both the ground of what matters and the music to accompany the discovery. In poems that by turns whisper secrets, belt out hard truths, and deliver lines like a shrewd stand-up comic, Erin Keane has put together a book that is as entertaining as it is compelling. What a fine mix of irreverence, insight, craft, and intelligence. *The Gravity Soundtrack* rocks."

—GREG PAPE, author of *American Flamingo* and Poet Laureate of Montana

"I've been a groupie of Erin Keane's poems for years and thought a full-length collection of her hip verses long overdue. *The Gravity Soundtrack* was worth the wait. Poem after poem here will make you smile, pause, think a little, feel like flirting. The pages brim with music and bourbon, myths and ghosts, a dreamy nostalgia for a past that never quite worked bolstered by a melancholic wish for a future that probably won't happen. Still, somehow, the rhythms swing and the pervasive feeling is buoyant celebration. These are poems that want to party! Keane has a sharp eye, a melodic ear, a sassy mouth, and a big ol' generous heart that keeps getting in the way. Nearly every one of her tunes sounds like a hit."

—GAYLORD BREWER

THE GRAVITY SOUNDTRACK

The Gravity
Soundtrack

‒‒‒∞∞∞‒‒‒

Erin Keane

For Becky —
I hope you enjoy
these words for your
With admiration for your
fine work —

WORDFARM
LA PORTE, INDIANA

WordFarm
2010 Michigan Avenue
La Porte, IN 46350
www.wordfarm.net
info@wordfarm.net

Cover Image: iStockphoto

Cover Design: Andrew Craft

USA ISBN-13: 978-1-60226-000-9
USA ISBN-10: 1-60226-000-1
Printed in the United States of America
First Edition: 2007

Library of Congress Cataloging-in-Publication Data

Keane, Erin.
  The gravity soundtrack : poems / Erin Keane.-- 1st ed.
    p. cm.
  ISBN-13: 978-1-60226-000-9 (pbk.)
  ISBN-10: 1-60226-000-1 (pbk.)
  I. Title.
  PS3611.E16G73 2007
  811'.6--dc22

                                                                    2007029170

P 10 9 8 7 6 5 4 3 2 1
Y 12 11 10 09 08 07

ACKNOWLEDGMENTS

Humble thanks to the editors of the following journals in which these poems, sometimes in different versions or under different names, first appeared:

Spoon River Poetry Review: "The Secret Garden," "Curious George," and "Little Women"; *Big Muddy:* "James and the Giant Peach," "Winnie the Pooh," and "The Velveteen Rabbit"; *Souwester:* "Peter Pan"; *Poems & Plays:* "The Jumbotron Nightmare" and "Aunt Molly's Advice to the Exhibitionist"; *Oyez Review:* "Science Fiction" and "Yellow"; *Floating Holiday:* "Charlie and the Chocolate Factory" and "Madeline"; *Riven:* "Sweet Aphrodite on a Bicycle"; *Arable:* "Butchertown Sabbath"; *The Heartland Review:* "In the Thorne Rooms at the Art Institute"; *Full Unit Hookup:* "The Angels' Share"; *Open 24 Hours:* "The Secondhand Record Store Clerk," "The One-Hit Wonders," and "Alice in Wonderland"; *Miller's Pond:* "Resident Alien"; *Strange Horizons:* "Orpheus Retires"; *New Southerner:* "*Priscilla Johnson* Still Has Hands Like Leaves"; *dComp:* "Germantown Prayer"; *Ariel:* "The Tao of Big Daddy," "Babar," and "The Nature of Our Looking."

"Orpheus Retires" also appeared in *The 2006 Rhysling Anthology,* published by the Science Fiction Poetry Association.

"*Priscilla Johnson* Still Has Hands Like Leaves" and "That Old Green Light" appeared in *New Growth: Recent Kentucky Writings,* an anthology of emerging Kentucky writers published by the Jesse Stuart Foundation in 2007.

The following poems were also published in a chapbook, *The One-Hit Wonders* (Snark Publishing, 2006): "Why We Do Anything," "The Postmodern Cowboy's Regret," "Some Nights," "Some Girls," "The Dead Letter Office," "Okay, I'm Invisible," "The Clash See the Future Recording *Give 'Em Enough Rope,*" "Things to Say When I Meet Shane MacGowan," "The Secondhand Record Store Clerk," "The Smallest Terminal," "The One-Hit Wonders," "Grievous Angel," "The Gravity Soundtrack," "Johnny Cash: Live Inside the Gates."

I'd like to give special thanks to my editor, Marci Rae Johnson, and Andrew and Sally Craft at WordFarm; to my mentors—Richard Cecil, Greg Pape, Jeanie Thompson, Debra Kang Dean, Kathleen Driskell and Molly Peacock—for their loving guidance and gracious support; to Richard Newman, Pam Steele, Frank X Walker, Jonathan Weinert, the She-Poets and the rest of the Pelican Mafia; to Rane Arroyo, especially; to the Kentucky Governor's School for the Arts; to Louisville at large and to my Monday nights and InKY; and to Beth Newberry, John Whitaker, and all my cousins, you softest shoulders.

For my families, both given and chosen

CONTENTS

Where there is sorrow, there is holy ground.
—Oscar Wilde, *De Profundis*

You keep eating your hand, you're not gonna be hungry for lunch.
—*The Breakfast Club*

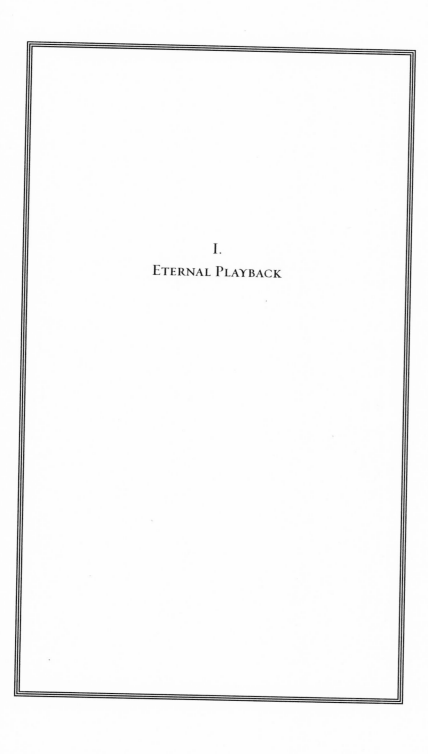

I.
Eternal Playback

The Gravity Soundtrack

Even now, grounded, a song scrap
drifting out a third-floor window
slips through the bare oak limbs,
firing memory: the skin on my back,
shag carpet, a tanktop. A car door
slams and I stop. Were we as thin

and quiet as I see us now through
my Vaseline lens? Me with long hair,
sprawled on your floor, cheap walls
pulsing with bass. Your wild head
an inch away, eyes on the ceiling,
painting in your mind. We were

scared, fatherless kids who couldn't
name the men we loved. We were
something like veal. Outside, a boy
snapped firecrackers, round after
round in the dry August night. You

cranked the volume. We wanted to
see how long we could hold our breath,
waiting, waiting, for spots in our eyes,
the burn in our bellies, for the slow
false rise from the floor, the lifting,
the dizziness that felt like floating.

The Clash See the Future Recording
Give 'Em Enough Rope

—London, 1978

Simonon's bored again, you know the look—deliberate
vacant, leg twitching, watching war films projected on the wall.

Blood-n-Guts Patton, *Paths of Glory.* Playing along
with machine gun blasts, he fucks up the take. 1977, the Jubilee,

over—that new band smell wore off. The Sex Pistols did it
first: paramilitary fashion's not enough, Paul's got to play

the damn thing right. Joe claims they're already legends. Well,
good thing—they'll be over in five. Strummer's going to die

at home with his dog, no blood on the sidewalk, only 20 footnoted
years of regret—long enough to hear heroin anthems pimp family

Caribbean cruises. A pause for all the beautiful jokes to come: the only
band that matters selling Jaguars, Baghdad burning to "Rock the Casbah."

The Tao of Big Daddy

His guitar groans "It's a Man's,
Man's, Man's World" and it

simply is. When Big Daddy
and The Kings of Love light

the backroom of Lisa's Oak
Street Lounge, wall panels

peel like tears. They, too,
are perfect, pockmarked

by dull switchblades. Your
intact skin, your wholeness

is not virtue. How could it be?
Big Daddy's furnace heart

flames. Furious fingertips, O
ten thousand nerves, a spark,

a bathroom wall's advice—
drugs before breakfast! or

take pills & die. The song,
yes, but Big Daddy too knows

hush: the lull in our constant
battled desire, the carved space

between *yes* and *no,* the empty
filled, finally, when we believe

in the complete, let go of the five
or so inches separating us all.

Things to Say When I Meet Shane MacGowan

I guess you're the incarnate redemption of every drunken Irish
    father: there's the dinner party story, where the host's baby wailed
a chesty yowl for parent or milk, and you rose from the table
    (barely propped on your elbows through dinner), cradled the tiny
        person
to your filthy shirt and sang "The Broad Majestic Shannon," the
        sweetest
    lullaby this side of daylight. At the end, the baby sighed, heavy
in your arms like a gift, and you laid it down in a cloud of duckie
        blankets
    then keeled over onto your face in the middle of the curious
        crowd. Still,

you greeted the millennium on stage and alive: more than we can say
    for my father, long since buried on Long Island, his contribution
to the people summed up in small donations to the IRA, in the
        shape
    of my brother's face. You couldn't save your front teeth, rotten
from abuse, and your beard stores the ashen flotsam of after-hours
        Dublin,
    yet you're beautiful, in the way that death-cheaters enjoy
an unnatural grace, in the way that "Dirty Old Town" pulls every
        maudlin
    gutstring. I'd like to say please don't think you'll be able to do this

for much longer, but maybe you can—and when you finally end up
        choking
    on your own vomit and meeting my dad in some afterlife poolhall,
he'll slap your back as he pumps your hand, and thank you loudly
    for keeping his little girl company. Confused, you'll flash that
        toothless
saint smile, stammer some wet-brained apology: *right, sorry and all,*

I could, y'know, have done more—of course you couldn't, of course he couldn't, it's okay, though, can I just say? Shane, I love you. I have all your albums.

The Secondhand Record Store Clerk

The clerk at Better Days knows
the location of each twice-loved album,
he can lay hands on *Dark Side of the Moon*
or *Beggar's Banquet* by closing his eyes
and trailing his fingertips along the cardboard edges
of the covers until his heart murmurs
and his hand knows this is the one.

The clerk at Better Days keeps time
by his piercings, knows that the first
eyebrow was for Julia when she left him,
the bar through his tongue to remind him
of the summer he said too much, each hole
in each earlobe growing larger to match
the years he's spent standing in the same spot.

The clerk at Better Days understands
your hunger for ten years ago, or twenty,
and knows that your high school reunion
is sneaking up and you need a copy
of *Bleach, Reckoning,* or *Let It Be* to feel
like a whole single person capable of dancing just
as badly as you did at the prom in rented shoes.

The clerk at Better Days can't name
the trees in Cherokee Park, doesn't know
the difference between a birch and an elm,
can't tell one nervous brown bird
from another, even when they nest in the eaves
above his window, and their babies grow
more hungry and bold by the day.

The clerk at Better Days runs fingers
through his hair, back to front, and sighs
with the weight of a complete discography, leans
elbows to countertop, silently counting
the tanks of gas it would take his ancient
Volvo to make it from this corner to
Miami, or New York, or San Francisco.

The clerk at Better Days ran out of breath
when he crossed the Mississippi and the land opened
like a book; driving I-70 west, he topped out
his lungs to a digital soundtrack, then whispered
into the canyons and let his voice bounce
off mountains that stretched skyward
in surrender, blood slowed to a trickle in his veins.

The clerk at Better Days lies down
during his lunch on the warm concrete and attempts
to hover using only the powers of his mind, tries
to harness this energy of the universe that he's heard
so much about, but grows sleepy and placid
as pedestrians step over him, the sun speckling
his lean torso between drifting clouds.

The clerk at Better Days climbs
onto his roof each night after the store closes
to count neon signs flickering
over Bardstown Road, ticks upcoming shifts off
in rhythm with the BIC lighter chorus
prowling, glowing the sidewalk below,
his own ashes tumbling into an empty soda can.

The Jumbotron Nightmare

Soon, after we have everything,
the electronic billboards will turn
on us. Last year's It Girl won't
wiggle her denim ass. Bud Light Beer
will not sponsor your outdoor
sporting event wedding proposal. Instead,

this will flash—pixels of you,
in ninth grade, telling that guy, his name
burned from your mental rolodex:
      you're a fucking loser.
Cut to his face. Part of you, maybe
just your pinky toe, will die
right there on the sidewalk. Then

the rapid eye movement scrapbook
of your little life so far: scorning, conning,
flinching, lying, immolating insects
with sunlight and a lens. Looped
on eternal playback, all PR stripped

for the city to see you—a peeled tangerine,
and you haven't moved since it started,
your eyes swirling like a hypnotized
cartoon, caught between Orwell
and Warhol: fingered and famous.

The Laff Box™

"This is the funny thing about laugh tracks: They work."
—The New York Times *on Charles Douglass, inventor (1910-2003)*

Even the weakest sitcom jokes have half
a chance with that bit of audience sweetening,
a social nudge to trigger our reluctant
response. Thanks to a lifetime of television's
prefab mirth, how will we still know funny
if we find it? I find myself, now, laughing

at the worst stuff—a barking, shocked noise,
alarming out loud: at a frog-eyed ingénue
mowed down by a speeding bus
in a stupid movie about death's tireless plan
to collect the check, at my friend Joe's
running gag about killing the dog next door
(ground glass in hamburger—*that's how
they do it on Staten Island*). In a more or less

inappropriate world, everything's funny,
or else nothing. What I need is a laugh track,
strapped to my person, constantly on,
to prompt and guide me, to let others know
when it's safe to laugh—a wink, a nudge,

then a low-voltage shock, for when we're deaf,
finally, to the roar of canned joy. Bury me
with my Laff Box, so I can keep on chuckling
right into the Afterlife—an endless marathon
of reruns, my classic episodes, the "Applause"
sign always lit, seasoned with just the right
timbre of giggle to encourage my decomposing
audience and the voracious, easily pleased worms.

Johnny Cash: Live Inside the Gates

A man spends a whole life getting ready
for Hell, then ends up here. A minute in this joint
feels like eternity—who can think straight
with "Air on a G String" hardwired in his ear?

And the floating, I may need a little time
to get used to it. A man wants solid ground
under his soles: reminds him where he came from,
and where he'll return—but this? I never seen
so many nuns and babies in all my life, and for once

I'm not hungry, or thirsty, or horny
or much of anything, but my fingers give off
a faint glow—it's spreading now to the crown
of my head, and I think I need to sit down, unless

I don't need anything anymore. June likes it,
she's bossing all the angels, but a man can't
settle for everlasting peace. Weightlessness
makes my head light—when you're looking

for the burn, burn, burn, and there's not even
harmonicas, what's left for a man? Nothing
ever happening, forever, strumming "Folsom Prison
Blues" on a tiny harp? Heaven's got nothing
on Tennessee. Now I got infinity left to go.

The One-Hit Wonders

We sit close on this cracked step and watch
the squirrels dance the autumn fugue, rational
on the surface but surely demented by the time
December shrills. They'll sleep, curled inside

dying trees, no memory of furious early
November. They would rather make it look
easy. Yesterday, I saw a fat one leap
to a far branch, and, missing, crash

through the tree, falling three stories
to the street. Stunned for only a beat, he stood
and ran back up the trunk. I don't doubt
who's favored—they run the neighborhood,

drunk on fermented nuts, that unseen hand
guiding their full bellies home, as we sit
on cooling concrete, pouring wine
and planning our futures, never as brilliant

as we were told we'd be. Tell me secrets—
who would you be if you could? Look at us
twitching inside our skins. Maybe only today
we can pretend our great expectations

still stand a chance. When morning rolls over
and gives the alarm clock the finger, throwing
the sun across the sky, the waning autumn light
will be erased, this last cigarette will vanish

from my hand. But here, now, nothing
tastes as sweet as virgin potential—fingerprint

smudged, but protected from measure. Remember
that, when we grow old and seasoned with envy,

stick it under your tongue. Keep it close like the final
unrequited love, like every scrap of slippery light
that will flash us awake, mouths dry and gaping, only
to fade to black, saving itself for another, quicker mind.

Orpheus Retires

Sons of muses know
the score—we follow,
heroic, in mother's footsteps.

It's duty, we're told. That's me
in the couplet, me the allusion,
a metaphor, a cipher: my name

carries weight. Personified
regret, I shorthand weakness,
and so am forced to relive

the worst day of my life
ad infinitum in the pages
of *Best American Poetry*.

What kind of afterlife
is this? Eternal humiliation
so another man won't

have to say *my love, I tried*
to save you, but I was stupid
and now you are lost. Enough.

Find another monkey, try
admitting your own faults
for a change. I'm heading

somewhere sunny, umbrella
drink in hand. Don't call. This time
there's no looking back, and

I'm taking Persephone with me.
Let the Pacific absorb our voices
into the pounding white noise waves.

The Smallest Terminal

Today, the gods of flight are laughing
at my turbo-prop plane—this little winged
coffin brooding on the tarmac,
metal staircase rattling in the breeze.
How many puny phobia incubators
will be swallowed by unforgiving
lakes and prairies before we go back
to trains? When I was young,
I thought only hicks were afraid
to fly. Small planes meant actually

feeling our way through the sky.
Turbulence? A chance to see someone
puke. Lately, only whiskey can get me
on board these anxious toy dogs,
and I can hear every screw loosen,
each lugnut rust. Ancient axles
and belts grind a *Lynyrd Skynyrd* chorus,
and we limp down the runway,
murmuring *Buddy Holly, Buddy Holly*.

Science Fiction

Last night, we watched the moon turn dark,
drank Rolling Rock on cobblestones. Little airplanes
fumbled through the clouds, eager for a look

at the eclipse. How carbon-based we are,
hair, some bone, mostly water. Small, plain,
last night, when we watched the moon turn dark

as morning on I-64: residents of the horse park
robed in mist like coddled bishops, their heads craned,
fumbling through the fog to sneak a look

at my Japanese death trap speeding to work.
And over this hill is another hill. The wax, the wane.
But last night, as we watched the moon turn dark,

I twitched, dumb-eyed, convinced some residual spark
might lift us over roof and brick. Of course we stayed
grounded: fumbling, human, dying for one quick look.

Luminous beings are we, not this crude matter—
lovely to believe, but this morning we are the same
as last night, when we watched the moon turn dark
and we gaped through the clouds, aching for a look.

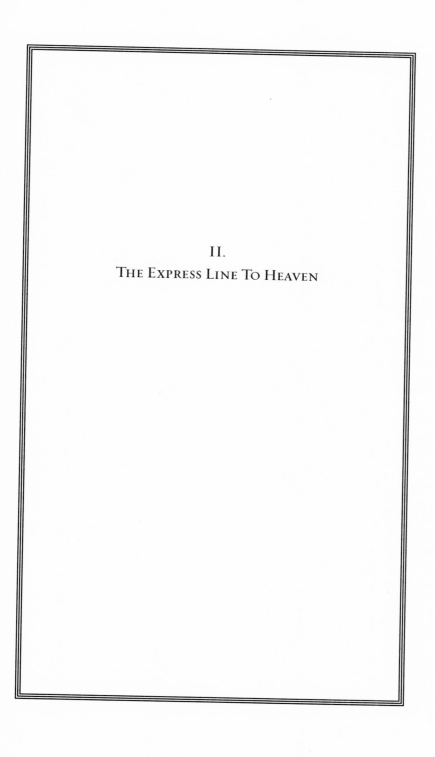

II.

THE EXPRESS LINE TO HEAVEN

That Old Green Light

All things pale & blooming with eyes sealed against
midday light. Playing coma never was such fun: night
creeps, the guestroom candle sputters. Might I be found
out. The day goes. The stars hide-and-seek with digital
bedside numbers, red blink vital signs in two/four time.
It is always midnight, if not noon. The downstairs party
swells, a beast, all murmur & assignation, so many
flowering branches artful in a vase: how some palms find

pliable waists to cup. Let fall the underwear like wilted
Kleenex. Stockings will crash on certain rumpled white
linens. Door ajar, my slant hall view. Voices lull & am I
the sole survivor? Breath held, believe that you might
climb the stairs in slow-mo, lit by trembling sconces,
full of nothing better to do, you emperor of this & that.

Sweet Aphrodite on a Bicycle

Drag your raggy ruffles
through the puddled gutter.
The gauzy tulle night wraps
over the French Quarter. It's never

quite dark, is it? Neon trashy
divas glow in doorways
and I wait in the corner
of this tiny decaying bar. You

cycle slowly through the window's
phantom lip smears. The low
clouds move faster than your legs
can pump. Over the slick

cobblestones, untied corset
ribbons brush the lamppost
and you're gone, mouthing couplets
into the fog. I close my eyes, inhale

your passing scent: bougainvillea
and mildew. By the river, a trumpet
sings, muted. Pocket change
rings the bottom of a coffee can.

The Angels' Share

It's what master distillers call the portion
that disappears from the barrels, lined up
and down the barn shelves: a whimsical,
prissy word for evaporation. Bourbon
ages in oak, absorbing, adding to
the flavor, but not replacing the sips
that slip down their ludicrous
throats. The more they take, the smoother
my drink—vanilla, wood, and fire—smelling
like Loretto when Heaven Hill burned,
a flaming river of whiskey licking

down the back roads. What order of angel
drinks Kentucky bourbon? Maybe the ophanim—
passed over for precious cherubim
and stuck-up seraphs, these middle children
are never tapped for guardianship. You won't
find one spilling out of a diaper, eye-
rolling through a portrait of some obscure
duchess, or drafted to fight anyone's
epic battles. Mascots of the cheerful

freeloader, the charming hustler, the good-
time gal, they weren't discovered in art
until tiny French Bohemian Toulouse
recognized their familiar red cheeks, smug
and beautiful, far from home. Perched
on barstools above the heads of ambersweet
men, they pierce smoke with sharp boot heels,
beaming through low light and cobalt glass.
The ethereal belles of last call twist scarlet
lips into rueful smiles, you know the ones

that say *we've been here for eternity,*
but it sure beats the other punishments.

Priscilla Johnson *Still Has Hands Like Leaves*

—after the painting by Alice Neel

Priscilla, by now you will have a Zoloft script that
won't quite do, a hypnosis tape
to cure that pack-a-day, some downtown boyfriend

Julian who will always be too
young for comfort, but he will be smooth,
Belgian, and you have had a thing

for Belgians since Richard's mother, the painter,
brought a poster back
from Brussells, a Bergman film with two

titles: *L'Oeil du Diable,*
Het Duivel's Oog. You considered—to have two
names, or two tongues: one

plush, one slender. Priscilla, you will still hate
The Beatles, but you'll like
that you're the only one. It is enough to love,

to nurture the small dislikes,
even this far from '66. And your clothes, they
will not have changed. Acid-

green shift, needing a steam in the worst way,
puddling on your sharp frame,
severe toes tipped like weapons: Italian leather

kitten heels pointy, tearing
up the carpet. You used to pose like a sour
Holly Golightly, one arm

vertical, wrist cocked, as if to wield a slim,
stemmed cigarette holder, but
you were 16, and even now, you still can't smoke

in front of anyone's mother.
So your thumb bent your middle fingernail
until it snapped, brittle snag

catching the upholstery. But, like now, you did not
care, in fact enjoyed leaving
a line of yourself traced in the arm of a chair.

To Melanín

When vanity snuck up on me, I looked
for you in the smooth, light length
of my legs and cursed the rainy DNA
that made me so white. You turned traitor
on me twice—transparent skin,
fair hair into dark. Stuck
in the land of no Irish, eclipsed
by UV fairies with atomic bikini lines
and state pageant wands, I burned red
every summer, peeling Book of Kells
parchment strips from my back.

You left me high and dry, no color
or glow, *the porcelain girl, she'll crack
if you drop her,* inking my face
warpaint blue to fight off the sun.
So thanks a lot, deadbeat pigment,
for Monicas and Renées screaming
you're so pale! and boys who tangled
their brown legs into mine,
comparing, seeing their reflections
in my stomach—me the ghost story,
and they breathless, afraid, chanting my name
three times fast into the sweet damp pillow.

Why We Do Anything

The glory and sigh
of the girls: gladiators
knew what guitarists

think they discovered.
Each lion killed rushes blood
to backstage cheeks, toes

curled, waiting to be
the reward. There can never
be enough but each

step on stage a chance
to graduate to god, take
what's rightfully theirs:

bodies dropping, tanned
offerings waiting to hear
you, and *you,* and *you.*

Body Shop: 3 A.M.

Sorry 'bout the nipples, guys—or rather,
the lack thereof. City requires pasties

if the girls get anywhere near you. Don't
look so disappointed. Will you settle

for Melody's g-stringed ass in your face,
rubbing in your hair? A peek down Amber's

pink pants? Brazilian wax—the express
line to Heaven. Slam a shot. Tip a buck.

Lean in, your girlfriend will never know. Lose
your fingers in the cleft of Charity's

crack of dawn. Tonight, it's okay to touch:
we know you expected more, that you came
in tasting hard pink pencil erasers.

Aunt Molly's Advice to the Exhibitionist

People are trying to fish here—take that
tackle downstream! Think of your grown children,
flipping through the night's news, TVs paused on
the station, their breath held in as they think
they recognize the shoes they bought for you
last Father's Day. *Did that blurred-out face kiss*
me good-night when I was five? your son will
wonder, and I will have to mention this
to Father Frank next Sunday. Do you think
you're the only one waiting for God's hand
to reach through heaven's gloryhole and
give you what you need? We all die alone,
you'll see, with our pants around our ankles—
just like you, now, with no hand save our own.

Some Girls

So we can shoot tiny cameras into bloodstreams, cure
hangovers and limp dicks with pills, and yet still no
prescription to keep my tongue in its own mouth all night—

volume turned up past decent, there's a pact I sign
in the moment when, faced with the veins in his arms
and my weak swear-off, it all falls apart. Because

something's damaged inside, they have to beat on
every surface—a sort of St. Vitus' Dance—and because
I know better. I've done this before: the yearning, it

never stops. You could meet halfway—we held back
those loaded nights. I could only be so tender. Like
babies, they break me, still, with one look. Like that girl,

I go back and back. Every time I trip over busted
mix tapes, there they are, each, one by one—in bursts—
curling half-smile—waxy hair—palming a drumstick,

breathing shallow and slow, tilting it left to right, never
looking down. I can still love the ones I never touched—
weirdly innocent. I couldn't smudge that delicate sepia

skin, not even when they would climb, separately then,
but now, in re-runs, in a relentless line, into the twin beds
of those years. They clung, I let them, it was all we could do.

The Equivalent of Ears

On our backs. Grass crawling bare
arms, the sweat sticking cotton

to skin & one-hundred-year
cicadas shatter-hulled beneath us

in the aerated soil. Wings reveal
single-letter communiqué: *W*, I want;

P, say please. Only the male of the species
can sing. We lie quite still. Clouds could

part like stage curtains, take us back
to re-naming all the lunar maria after

inkblots in our CAT-scanned heads.
Sea of Senility. Ocean of Ice Cream

Trucks. Still, the covered moon. Exo-
skeleton crunch. Like us, they were

grubs in the dirt before this. Night
cups you in warm wax after all

day in the pre-tornado calm. So many
craters face away. What is there

to get back to? There is only studying
and more naming of rightful names.

Your hand flutters, a laced wing
on a single breeze-shuddered leaf.

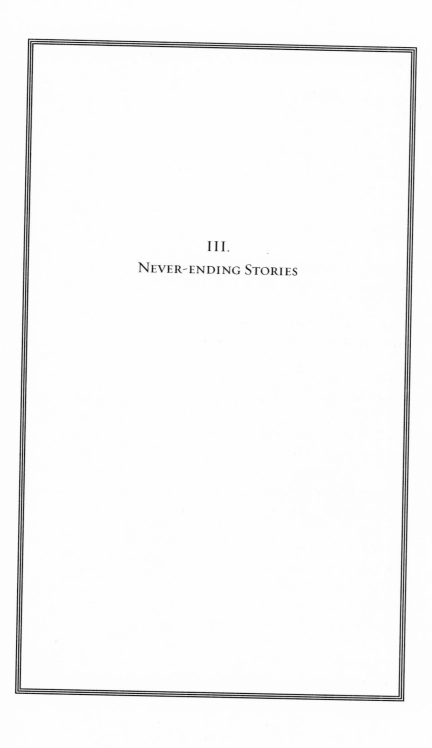

III.
Never-ending Stories

The Secret Garden

When there is nobody left, if a parent
or two should die, all you need is a project
to keep you busy. Maybe a garden, maybe
a melancholy uncle who needs cheering.
When you're small, days unravel,
until one day it's April again
and you're digging a hole in your backyard
for a patio and planting beds. You shovel

up all of spring's mess (the mud, the worms),
dodging caterpillars who are marching in great
numbers. You're shoveling against the sun.
Artifacts unearthed, catalogued: a porcelain
doll's head, broken at the neck; a yellow
Matchbox taxicab, wheel missing; several marbles,
chipped, dirt-caked. At the end of the day,
you drink screwdrivers in spite of your ulcer, polish

the cats-eye on your jeans and eyeball
your stripped yard. There's no wall around it, just
a chainlink fence that won't block nextdoor's
dog stench. There's no manor house on the moor,
just Yellow Cab Dispatch across the alley,
and it is Easter, but as we all know,
there's no big miracle, no empty tomb, only
your shovel, your mud, your marbles, your worms.

Little Women

Just what in the hell was wrong with Beth,
anyway? As far as any fourth-grader could tell,
she died of boredom, a short lifetime on the couch
spent diddling her kittycats, applauding Jo's
gender-benders. Arty types always identify

with Jo—we assistant editors, we grant-
beggars who drag our bewildered, weird
husbands around, symbols of our adorable
eccentricities. And the less said

about Meg, the better. In another book,
she'd have made a champion suburban
carpooler, regulating sugar and schedules,
hiding tiny cuts in her forearms
under a polyknit sweater. Oh, Beth,

did the pressure to be good ever get so bad
that you let your translucent hand linger
just a moment too long on the minister's
worsted arm? You should have pulled Laurie
down on that couch some delirious
afternoon (when you knew Amy would walk in
so she'd always know you'd had him

first), then brushed off the cat hair and grabbed
the first train to New Orleans. You would have
loved it, Beth: the pipe-smoky dancehalls,
piano-playing Creole lovelies with whiskey-
flavored tongues whispering *mon petit moineau*
up your arched neck. For all of us, Beth—to hell
with charity, Marmee, and *Pilgrim's Progress*:
here we go again, another Young Girl Classic.

Where the Wild Things Are

We have been abandoned. All night
the wild rumpus raged for our king.
As sudden as Max came, he left.

It is not so bad, a monster's life.
There's the odd terror, the marrow
slurped from shattered tibias. Still,

we hear things. Hairy scary brutes.
Nightmare wall shadows. Godzilla
and Tokyo. We know, we know.

We need a leader. Why not footie
pajamas? We picked him from all
the sleeping little boys. An honor.

To go home to his mommy when
we gave him a crown. To do what
we cannot. He did not belong?

He is wild thing enough. Tiny,
yes. But fiendish under pink skin.
One day, he will return, like all.

Then, we will show him monster.

The Little Prince

It's a terrible job I have, trust me.
What use is a streetlamp on a planet

this small? Days and nights blur
and I spin a little faster on my toothpick

axis, drawing lost children like moths
seeking something larger than themselves.

It's a tiny rock, kids, and I am the worst
of fools: function without form, unable

or unwilling to put down my tools. What else
could I be? All you believe in is the sun,

endless possibility, constant light. What I
know is work: expectations never quite

filled. Don't ask me to save you. Move on
with the scholars of eternal things, leave

the ephemeral where you find it: under
glass—captured, frozen, loved to pieces.

Curious George

Say you're a little monkey, kicking
around the forest with your monkey pals,
and from nowhere, this guy lures you in
with a big yellow hat, grabs you from
behind with a potato sack. *Naughty?*

You tried jumping ship. Dumbass
calls you curious. He's keeping
his silly little monkey! Just your luck.
What does the big yellow hat do
for a living, anyway? You're starting

to suspect he doesn't work for the World
Wildlife Foundation. When he squeezed
your furry torso into a t-shirt made
for a boy, the jig was up. Here's Gepetto
with an ape. Your name is no more

George than his is Kong, but tell that
to the guy walking you into stores like
management won't care. The way he looks
at you, Jesus, like a bad kid on Christmas
morning: greedy, proud. Look! He's got

a monkey! You pretend to be asleep
when he climbs into your bed some nights,
breath deep, measured, trying not to squirm
as he nuzzles his face into your fur. You're
frozen—he picks nits of love off your back.

Charlie and the Chocolate Factory

What they didn't tell us, after we unwrapped
the lucky bar, was our place in the plot: stupid,

fat, competitive, spoiled—at a madman's whim.
We were to make the blond kid look good

by comparison—he only had to top our
dubious virtue. Shooting fish in a stockpot!

There's a special place in Hell reserved for
people who tempt small children with rivers

of chocolate and drown them while they drink.
Olympic cruelty—I am waiting for the irony

to stop: let us, the greedy brats, gather our spoils
to our chests. Let there be no correction tonight.

Let the good kid kneel beside his crippled elders
and massage their gouty legs, forgetting to remind

us all of his sacrifice. Let him bless their bunions.
The lazy, the conniving, the slow—we've gathered

outside the factory gates. The sweet-tart rejects
have come home, Wonka. We would like our reward.

Babar

As if enough weren't enough, now even elephants
hate the French. Colonialist bullets killed Babar's
parents, painted over his life with gentle watercolors:
tailored suits, chandeliers. There's no money in noble
savagery—today, Louis Vuitton sends pachyderm-
sized handbags for the missus. *Pâté* and *chocolat*
pool like chunky primordial soup around his stumpy
feet, still unused to carpets, destroying champagne
brunch with an impatient stamp. Babar remembers

life before civilization: little birds on his back to pick
out the gnats. O the days of un-styled hair! To lurch
into a mud wallow, scratching his underbelly against
the rough earth. To be male and whole, extending
unfettered toward the ripe orange sun. He tries
in the drawing room, and the servants titter behind
their hands. Slumping onto the fainting couch, he nods
at the valet. Edith Piaf pours over him, her life in pink
vowel-rich and glossy through the vinyl static crackle.

James and the Giant Peach

James ran away in a big piece of fruit:
the beginning of the story. That is,
he has a dangerous past. A wanted boy.
Like Candy, like the Sugar Plum Fairy,

James came to New York, moved into a pit
of an apartment and became fabulous.
When he walked down the street at dusk,
stoopsitters lifted their chins with hydraulic

fists and muttered damp appreciation
for his fine self. That is, he became a wanted
boy: rags became costumes on his clothes-
hanger frame, shoulders twisted, a perpetual

25-degree-angle. A hat pulled down over
his face, one eye squinting. Boots. Downbeat
everyone can hear. He dances after hours,
beloved of djs who play his favorites,

tears smudging eyeliner. Footprints in
glitter. Still, by dawn, tripping out
onto the street he can feel himself sinking,
little by little, smelling the fishy breath

of the sharks, which the boys in the club
believe to be metaphor. It can't be anything
like gliding straight over the white cliffs, like
splashlanding in the Atlantic. What could he

do but whisper *ladybug, grasshopper, spider*
like a prayer? It's not for us to judge. He was

a wanted boy on the tip of the Empire State Building:
blood staining cheeks, so full, pink, juicy, fresh.

Alice in Wonderland

Eat Me, Drink Me—that kid would put anything
in her mouth. Alice grew up, got high singing
"Baba O'Riley" behind a towering
set of Midwest stadium bleachers, sped
a Camaro out of town with the oldest guy
left in school. Now she waits tables, drives
customers crazy with questions: the duck, sir,
an excellent choice, but wouldn't one prefer
the duck? She likes the thirsty, mad men—
the one they call *untouchable,* she calls

mine—who will jump for the hell of it
into her, touching and rearranging
as they fall, shrugging through a bottomless
hole narrow as a set of shoulders, chewing
both sides of the mushroom just to keep
up. In the mirror, Alice practices a smile
so horrible it makes the rest of her body
disappear, and at night, the cards leap

into her hands. She shuffles like a pro, following
each ugly face through the deck, can stop
on command and name the next number.
Alice carries a gun these days—delicate,
pearl-handled but loaded just the same—
shoots public park squirrels out of trees,
whispers *they ask for it, they ask for me by name*
out of the corner of her sly grinning mouth.

Heidi

The highways between my mother's house
and mine are littered with plastic shrines
to eternal teenagers, dead on prom night
or after the Big Game: weathered teddy bears,

handlettered prayers wrapped in plastic, guilty
flowers dropped by a luminous class secretary.
The lucky survivors get twisted into human
pretzels, forever encased in metal, spinal cords

tinfoiled into a wad of ninety-miles-an-hour
and the perfect radio song. Far from wealthy Clara,
there's no spa cure, no pigtailed orphan hired
to buck them up. They sit. Some squeak rubbertire,

some whirr softly by in a motorized whiff
of mall counter perfume. Maybe all I can see
is a seventeen-year-old's collapsed eye socket,
five years of sacrificial orthodontia shattered

through a skeleton smile. These are not imaginary
ailments, so no alpine heroine's cult of personality
can sweep down the mountain and convince
them they can walk. All we have is our height,

more than five feet off the ground, to stare over
their heads. We can't bring back our dead fathers
by healing them. So we eat some more goat cheese.
So we plan a Swiss backpacking trip for the summer.

Winnie the Pooh

If you are, among your friends and relations,
a Rabbit (or worse, an Owl), get used to hiding
your disappointment. You know you can't
call Eeyore to pick you up when your car
goes dead during rainy rush hour: *you think*

you're having a shitty day? and the litany
of company-loving misery follows. Piglet's
not taking his meds, you know the agoraphobia,
but he knows you can take care of it since
you are so well put-together and did you
know that he feels very small today? Every day

he says it—cute Piglet, so tiny and wobble-
headed it's a wonder he hasn't met the business
end of a slobbering wolf. List the stuff that will
make him strong: yoga, a housepet, aromatherapy.
Let him whimper on the other end, sink deeper
into your seat. You've nowhere to go but home,
where seventeen messages beep from Tigger,

bouncing off his ass all day with the next
Big IDEA! caffeinatedcontactlenssolution!
This is what he does instead of work. You will
pour shots tonight to rein him in—if you can ever
get a ride home. A last resort, you dial dopey down-
stairs neighbor Pooh, hoping he can find the phone
under the stacks of take-out boxes and newspapers.
You hear a muffled *aw, bother* after he drops
his phone. You hear it every night in your sleep,
not sure if those three sonorous beats echo
in your mind or if he's really up all night, hitting

his head against the wall over and over, stumped
by the doorknob. Still, he's your favorite of the fragile,
for the sweet dry-rot stuffing smell that reminds you
of your mother, last seen sniffing once again
around the wrong farmer's kitchen garden, leaving
you in charge. You notice Pooh hasn't said *hey man*
or *wanna order a pizza* yet, and those involuntary

muscles in your chest clench. You breathe slow
to stop the mental slideshow—aneurysms, bee
attacks, a falling piano—*pick up the phone.* Does
he have his inhaler? *Pick up the phone.* He's just
distracted. But now you're whispering. *Pick it
up.* You can't help it. Your mouth aimed away
from the receiver, eyes on your watch. On five
you'll hang up. *Pick it up.* On ten. Fifteen. Twenty.

Madeline

What's a girl got to do around here
for a little attention? Three years since
he dumped me in this hellhole, not even
so much as a visit. Sure, the other girls and I,
we have some good times—ice skating outside
the Hôtel de Ville, the time Inspector Feaufrou
chased a jewel thief through the Place Vendôme—

but what about his promises? The Louvre,
well, there's no time, between the teeth-brushing
and the marching in two straight lines. Always
in formation, little soldiers in the war against
bad manners, and Papa in London with Chantal,
playing *financier et secretaire.* Boredom school,

more like it, can you blame me for faking?
The doctor was easy, a pint
of Miss Clavel's aged scotch
and he would have called the Pope
for me, and when the ambulance
screamed past the Eiffel Tower, cutting
the smudgy night with high beams, I knew
they'd put me under the knife and he'd have
to come. I yelled holy bloody murder,
clutching my stomach—a worthy

performance. Counting backwards
from one hundred, breathing the gas,
two straight lines of nursemaids marching
across my closed eyelids, twelve little
fathers boarding twelve little trains
for Paris. The next day, I woke

to a dozen frothy pink roses
at my bedside, *Get well, ma cherie!*
typed on the card. The girls showed up,
went gonzo over the dollhouse, jump ropes,
and bonbons—his long-distance bribes. What

did they know of holiday weekends
in the kitchen with the one cook on duty?
Hands curled into fists, I dug my fingernails
into whitened palms, smiling like I wanted

what I got. Let them play with his
guilty trash. A phantom pain shot
through my stomach. Lips stretched
in a tight line, I stood on the bed,
commanding them closer, to see up close
what they came for. I pulled the shirt up—
a balloon-red scar tracked across my belly,
stitched shut with black thread. This,
at least, is mine. I have earned it.

Peter Pan

If an androgynous waif in tights should fly
through your window some windy night promising
a gravity cure, replace the locks right away. Don't
think your racing pulse is nature's encouragement.
He's not looking for a new love, baby: these lost
boys need mommies for empty pedestals, for mending
their holey psychic pants all the night long. At first,

you might feel chosen, like only you could fix
his supposed broken self. But there's no dealing
with boys who won't grow up. Of course
he will disclose in his novel the precise
details of each of your breakups, and the time
you found him at four in the morning on your
best friend's front yard putting out
cigarettes on his forearm. That will be your fault,
along with the rest. Pirates? Don't fly. Some
have hooks for hands. But try one, let the curve

of stainless steel brand the small of your back,
let him call you his worthy adversary. Let the foam
hiss of the surf spray your cheek as your toes test
the spring of the plank; let his spidery lace cuffs,
speckled with the blood of last night's victim, curl
around your waist from behind; let the thick smell
of gunpowder and sweat coat your skin. Say
goodbye to smooth foreheads, untouched
by the world—let the crocodile circle the ship,
ticking in time with your ragged, baited breath.

The Velveteen Rabbit

What good is it to be real? By the time it happens,
you've lost your looks, the plush belly you were so
proud of, the pink nose he kissed lightly before
bedtime. You figure, if you hang around long enough,

maybe you'll transform before your eyes fall out,
before your sawdust innards break open on Candyland,
coating Gumdrop Mountain in flaky guts. All you ever
wanted was a mechanical inside, with a crank to wind

your springloaded legs up, up, up! so you could hop
out of his arms and into the bush. The last he
would see of you—a dandelion puff tail, twitching
sayonara to the heavy down comforter, the thumb-

sucking, the snot. Tossed out with the trash, then
it happened, and you knew before you reached
a real toenail to your real, itchy nose: the silvery
shimmer of doubt crept up your throat. So much

for the great escape. You've outrun his regrets, now
you're stuck with this fragile, tense body. Feeling
the wind chill for the first time, you know: welcome
to the absolute, to the quickening, to the becoming.

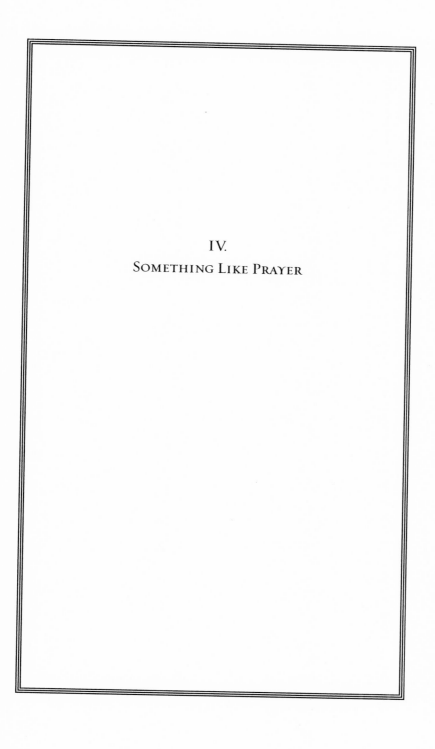

IV.
SOMETHING LIKE PRAYER

The Postmodern Cowboy's Regret

The world wants nothing more than for us to stay forever
in this moment: immobile on a rented bedspread, facing

generic lithographs with cocked grins, loaded eyes. If we mean
what we say, we'll both vanish by sunrise. If we say what we

mean, sweat will scrape into every new cut, our nails bitten
down to the quick. Songs will write themselves. Six cylinders wait

for my clutch, shift—give me a mechanical bull, eight seconds
pass in a blink, but this eternity in a yes or no—I almost leave,

a silhouette riding into storm-heavy clouds—then your finger
traces the seam of my jeans, up past the point of *Sweet Jesus*.

From a Colorado Giftshop

The air is thin here, so close
to the sun. Skin can burn
in a minute. At the top

of Lookout Mountain is
Buffalo Bill's grave, a creepy
wishing well, a shrine littered

with coins tossed by pilgrims
in frontier drag. They trekked
up in minivans and motorcycles

to roleplay their respects.
A game as old as the West—
cowboys and Indians. Sure,

we're still paying for the past, and
it's never enough, these few
coins from little boys' pockets.

From here, you can see Denver.
The city's in drought, each thunder
cough stops us cold like an awkward

attempt at conversation. The air
hangs heavy around our necks
like leaden medicine bags,

or a hundred personalized tin
marshall stars strung on the sale
rack: Joshua, Emily, Daniel, Marie.

Germantown Prayer

Blessed Virgin of the Garden Gnomes,
keep the order of chainlinked frontyards
chrysanthemum-safe and fast. Gather

your concrete children in the belly
of the flight path, this consecrated
urban ground. Pilgrims in black eyeliner

and rolled skirts, the schoolgirls are on
the move, playing passion in the nowhere
hours of dwindling afternoon. Our Lady of

Perpetual Rent Checks, know us now
and in the brief hour of our lawn mowing,
cats ghost-printing the hoods of previously-

owned cars, babies dandled on porch swinging
knees. Waiting for annunciation, the flashbulb
second when everything changes—but I am

not alone. Holy Painted Mother, bless our
camelbacks and foursquares, these optimistic
windchimes, your oldest faithful, the new blood,

your coveralls and ties, swallows and sea
monkeys alike. Lead us out of the holding
pattern, into a pinhole snapshot of what is

to come: a creeping shadow circle, the blessed
who and the sacred with, the where and under
cool plaster hands—the grace, the finally, the when.

The View Below Sea Level, November

From the wrought-iron railing, the heat and the damp
eat a house in rapid time-lapse. Vines choke the hollow
second floor, while the roof, caved in three places,
stutters through the fog. I sip coffee, watch a brick

crumble, compare the temperature to home. My
nomadic future: New York for fall, here in the tropics
by December, summers in the west of Ireland—Galway,
Connemara, the Gaeltacht—impossibly lush, benign.

Spring could happen in Prague, Missoula, Kent.
Really, does it matter? Everywhere the frantic rebirth,
the drizzle, the fertilized garden stink. In a perfect world,
March will take me to Australia—skip spring, get twice

the autumn: moldy lawn-waste fires, cut-glass daylight,
bloodorange leaves. On the other side of the world, time
swirls counterclockwise, and I am small again, whole,
running footraces against the rotation of the Earth.

Yellow

Like amber with the blood sucked out. July
in heatwave flame. Walking down the stained

East Village sidewalk, littered filter tips
remind me: once, before I was, my parents

lived here. Just a gleam in daddy's eye. His ghost
plays cards on fire escapes. Like always,

I remember him with light washed pale behind,
corona bright around his head. The tricky

memory of childhood. Scenes stick, color
fades. This tint says thumbprint, albums,

Kodak. East Coast blurred to Southwest
backyard sand. A half a world from home,

the eerie winter heat bleached months
as blank as empty lamplight. I held my breath

and snapped the tails off lizards. *Wait,* he said,
for Easter. See you, turning monochrome.

Resident Alien

The little that I know of the suburban
Midsouth sleeps in the hills we'd jump
in secondhand cars, in the meter of lawn
sprinklers ticking up County Line Road.

I lived there, that's all. There was a boy.
There was always a boy. He could fish,
knew how to start fires in the mosquito
woods along the lake. When he pushed

me against a swimming pool wall in July,
our feet—treading, wrinkling—tangled
underwater. I tasted his toes, one by one,
suckling chlorine and salt. I let my tongue

trap me. We went back to his trailer, laid
still, stiff. Nerve gone. Rain tapdanced
the roof. Midsummer loomed, and I didn't
know I couldn't be from there anymore:

from the quick slip into the amniotic pool,
from the glowing blue bottom tiles, the wet
limbs and the landscape lighting trembling
off the slow rippling surface of the water.

Butchertown Sabbath

The light sulks through gaps in your vertical blinds;
your full-body stretch assures you nothing's broken.

Sweet hangover—last night's forbidden smoke still
in your throat, and your leg thrown over his long, snoring body,

and work a full twenty-four hours away. Against reason,
you still sleep in a kingsized waterbed, and it swells

and laps with each headscratch, each half-roll, like being past
the surf in the ocean. Every hour, you wake, stare

at the clock, go back to sleep. By eleven, the pet rooster
across the street stirs—he's a city animal, rarely crows

before noon on Sunday. Another semi downshifts
around the suicide curve, its live cargo slammed

into the stainless steel corner, and the thrill is too much
for the pigs. They scream like it's a rollercoaster.

On Childlessness

This was when we lived in a crumbly
second-story shotgun
and leaving for a week we turned off
the window air-conditioning unit.
Yes, we boiled our frog. He was ours,
we hated him. Fat little albino
murdered his tankmates
and had no personality. We ignored him

and he grew, stuffing infrequent food pellets
with tiny claw-tipped fingers
into his leering mouth.
His last year he clammed up
and refused to sing. That
was that. For conservation,
safety, and thrift we flipped
the switch and hit the road. Look,
we're not monsters. Please do not alert

People for the Ethical Treatment of Animals.
Being cold-blooded
we guessed he would adapt
to rising temperatures. Truth
is we came home to ten gallons of rotting mess
and an ex-amphibian floating
on top, and what's worse
we left the horrible tableau
on display for over a week
until the former Mr. White broke
into several diaphanous pieces,
fluttering bits of skin waving at us

through algae-chunked aquarium glass,
each waiting for the other to make the first move.

The Dead Letter Office

They don't exist on paper, no blue ink snaking
over the page like spider veins, like tributaries
of a greater river. These letters sit, shifting weight
from side to side, left-brain to right-, wanting
postage, heavy stationery, embossed or hand-
stamped, to be wrapped in thick envelopes

that say *this is important, listen.* Once in a while,
each can feel the weight of a hand, intentional,
pressing, taking its pulse. One knows a guitar string
callus that protects a fingertip from slicing open
over lined notebook paper, writing its own version
of midnight: one uniquely flawed print to another,

a message from the twenty-four-hour confessional.
Another welcomes the smudge of dirt from a thumb
that plants bulbs in October, waiting for the payoff—
April reds and yellows—but uncertain, one shaky eye
on the frost. The oldest letter folds and refolds itself
a million times a day, memorizing the crease pattern,

knowing that nobody will be coming for it any time
soon, but ready, always ready. If they took form,
they would cover every surface, rough and smooth,
words small at first, then bolder with every loop
and dash. Each knows exactly what it would say:
the undeliverable, the invisible between the lines.

Okay, I'm Invisible

So what now? The locker room at the YMCA
only took a half hour, and I've spied on the mohawk'd
guy I followed home for the last 45 minutes
but all he's done is listen to "Stairway to Heaven"
on repeat, scratching his belly plateau, slowly, free thumb
hovering near the shuffle button on the remote
in case his sneering housemates arrive. Am I wasting

my time? I should be saving babies, kittens, maybe
I'll head down to the grade school, leave the back door open
for a three-legged dog. Minor mischief and misdemeanor
peeping: I'm useless. I move closer, his head is weaving

with the chorus, Marlboro smoke swirling through
the dark spikes of his hair. Up close, his face creases
with the late hours of shift work, his van
on cinderblocks. I am on his lap.
All superhero, I try to think of where my hands
might do some good, might remind him of being

seventeen in a backseat with Alexis from homeroom
popping Bubble Yum in his speakershot ears, might
make him think it's all lewd slowdances,
it's all Led Zeppelin in a basement with your
headphones on. The song picks up tempo
and I am magnificent and delicate like a surgeon.
He thinks it's just the song bouncing off
scratched hardwood floors, the late afternoon
shining sweetly through the blinds.

Some Nights

Choked as we were by the damp, buggy air, we reached
across the railroad tracks, stoplights, and corner markets

that fell along the streets between us and turned on
each other's radios: we had entire frequencies to ourselves.

For you, a crackling AM pirate station, static humming
underneath your private playlist, the DJ dedicating

torch songs to every girl you used to crawl across
in the early hours of after-work glow—the sweet

self-torture, you couldn't turn it off, only rubbed
your head, walked the floor like a guard. For me,

there were no station breaks. The switch you flipped
flooded my head with the longest instrumental ever

recorded, all languorous jangle and blurry wail, until
it was all I could hear, it was all songs and all sounds.

Even after you pulled the cord, I could still hear it across
runoff rainwater and moths attacking streetlamps—

tuning your guitar, you blew smoke through the window screen,
through my fingernails trailing across the fine, dense mesh.

The Nature of Our Looking

—after the film by George and Gilbert

A piano tinkles: it's faraway black & white times,
boisterous, a dancehall rag—but every mannered
Dunhill drag breaks the pose. A cocked knee, a chin
pointing to what should be marked: an archetypal
riverbank afternoon. Respects must be paid.
The reclining young men know, and they
whisper with every flickering frame: nothing
was better back then. Only your yearning thrives.

In the dark room, we watch. Some modern truth
suggests we could be videotaped and projected
onto a wall in another part of town, or preserved
for the next generation to mock: voyeurs, seekers,
live sculptures in a gallery landscape, peeling back
layers of the joke to find the coiled infinite inside.

In the Thorne Rooms at the Art Institute

Collected in a tucked-away
museum corner, these little scenes
are a stalker's love letter.
Some demented genius
shrunk the bedrooms, parlors,
kitchens of every American era
and created a miniature
furniture zoo—once-proud
chippendales, hepplewhites—
ever-red apples never rot
on matching walnut end tables.

There's a rail for the devoted
to kneel on and whisper
into freeze-dried domestic
aquariums. Go ahead and pray
to the god of diminutive order,
warm the glass with abbreviated
psalms because the exhibit
is empty, the rooms still,
meticulous, waiting for just one

mini-American to return home
for his 5 o'clock ritual:
put his feet up, turn on the hi-fi,
grammophone, or player
piano and plot an escape
from his perfect airless home.

A Divine Infestation

I. THE LITTLEST ONE INTERRUPTS

He wanted a place to sit. Bulky jacket pulled
close around shoulders, stained Yankees cap
tight on his ears. There's room: you never know
when a messenger could arrive in disguise. He smelled
our need to be liked, to be thought kind, and soon
we're buying him beers, begging Lucky Strike
redemption, until he starts throwing glass ashtrays
and a big guy headlocks him, tossing him onto the lamplit
sidewalk. It was then we noticed the new faces
in the crowd, but nobody wants to be the first
to point out the twitching shapes of their jacketed
backs and too-casual poses, or the way their disturbing
eyes followed the banished one—he'd claimed
to be a runaway from Las Vegas (of all things and places).

II. THE FLASHY ONE GRINS, UNFORTUNATELY

We're not even supposed to be talking about
him. We are afraid of betraying nonbeliefs. Still,
he dazzles. The fifteen seconds he spent standing
beside the bar, tapping his foot, swirling the ice
in his glass, felt like a week. On cue, the jukebox
fell silent. Nobody could explain the burning
in our toes, the prickly sensation of being
in the presence of another, higher order. He says
so where are you going tonight? but we hear
why are you favored with free will, sex, and death?
and when he smiles at us, his face doesn't wrinkle,
his teeth blind and accuse. We tried to ignore him,
but couldn't take our eyes off his wings folding
and unfolding, slowly (he says it's a reflex).

III. The Tattooed One Tends Bar

It's a siege—they've taken the castle, we've grown
accustomed to the telekinesis and the halos. They know
now we can't stay away, and they must have
their own reasons for not going back. But if
you ask, you'll receive. Bourbon, vodka, gin dance
from his scarred divining rod fingers. Cherries
jump in your glass on command. He tends our guilt
and suspicions, stokes our regret, points to
ancient scriptures inked up and down his marble arms,
and we almost stop flinching when he leans in
to light our cigarettes. The secret: he can be bribed.
Every extra dollar secures a word upstairs, a reassuring
and devastating smile. We tip over and over. Something
like prayer spills out of us (it's what he lives for).

Grievous Angel

Who's to say what's serious, a joke made
at the edge of a friend's grave? A promise.
The desert, a gas can, a light. A corpse

has no value, you'll only be charged
with coffin theft: a misdemeanor, a prank,
setting a body on fire. My bodysnatcher,

my brother, haven't we done this, already,
too many times? The many ways to scatter
a burden: hot ash wind lifting like a UFO's

beam, lizards tracking me, charred, through
the Joshua Tree sand. The left bits swept up,
mailed to New Orleans, God's own singer

put down near the highway. A laugh, at last:
ours—I rest here. Me reflected in your pupils,
orange, blossoming. I couldn't give you

anything to hold, so take this wakeful night,
know it can't make sense. What's left? At least
make it a good story. An offering, one last.

NOTES

"The Tao of Big Daddy" is for Jeffrey Lee Puckett.

"Things to Say When I Meet Shane MacGowan": the dinner party story is apocrypha, but highly probable.

"Science Fiction": the quotation in this poem is by Yoda, from *The Empire Strikes Back*. This poem is for Amy Clark.

"The Equivalent of Ears": There are no 100-year cicadas, but if there were, they would be even louder than 17-year cicadas, which can produce rattling sounds up to 106 decibels. While only male cicadas can produce that sound, both sexes have membranes that function like ears.

"Why We Do Anything": the quotation in this poem is from gladiator graffito found on the Coliseum in Rome.

"Some Girls" is for Terri Whitehouse.

"From a Colorado Giftshop" is for Emily Tryer and Dan Stokes.

"In the Thorne Rooms at the Art Institute": The 68 Thorne Miniature Rooms at the Art Institute of Chicago depict elements of European and American home interiors from the late 13th century to the 1930s.

"Grievous Angel": Country-rock pioneer Gram Parsons died of an overdose of alcohol and morphine at 26. At fellow musician Clarence White's funeral in 1973, Parsons told his friend and road manager Phil Kaufman that he wished to be cremated in Joshua Tree National Monument, where he often spent weekends. Later that year, after Parsons' death, Kaufman stole his body from the Los Angeles Airport, where it awaited shipment back to New Orleans for burial, and set him on fire in the California desert. Kaufman was arrested, but fined only $700 for the theft of the coffin.